A Guide to
AMERICAN STATES

Wisconsin

THE BADGER STATE

MEDIA ENHANCED BOOKS
AV2
BY WEIGL
ADDED VALUE • AUDIO VISUAL

www.av2books.com

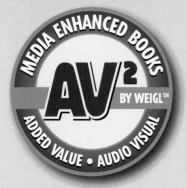

AV² provides enriched content that supplements and complements this book. Weigl's AV² books strive to create inspired learning and engage young minds in a total learning experience.

Your AV² Media Enhanced books come alive with...

Audio
Listen to sections of the book read aloud.

Key Words
Study vocabulary, and complete a matching word activity.

Video
Watch informative video clips.

Quizzes
Test your knowledge.

Go to **www.av2books.com**, and enter this book's unique code.

BOOK CODE

B 9 2 3 4 6 5

Embedded Weblinks
Gain additional information for research.

Slide Show
View images and captions, and prepare a presentation.

AV² by Weigl brings you media enhanced books that support active learning.

Try This!
Complete activities and hands-on experiments.

... and much, much more!

Published by AV² by Weigl
350 5th Avenue, 59th Floor
New York, NY 10118
Website: www.av2books.com   www.weigl.com

Library of Congress Cataloging-in-Publication Data

Parker, Janice.
 Wisconsin / Janice Parker.
    p. cm. -- (A guide to American states)
 Includes index.
 ISBN 978-1-61690-823-2 (hardcover : alk. paper) -- ISBN 978-1-61690-498-2 (online)
 1. Wisconsin--Juvenile literature. I. Title.
 F581.3.P373 2011
 977.5--dc23
                    2011019239

Printed in the United States of America in North Mankato, Minnesota

052011
WEP180511

Project Coordinator Jordan McGill
Art Director Terry Paulhus

Photo Credits
Every reasonable effort has been made to trace ownership and to obtain permission to reprint copyright material. The publishers would be pleased to have any errors or omissions brought to their attention so that they may be corrected in subsequent printings.

Weigl acknowledges Getty Images as its primary image supplier for this title.
Photo of Abraham Lincoln Presidential Library and Museum on page 20 courtesy of Edward A. Thomas.

Contents

The skyline of Milwaukee features modern skyscrapers and the Milwaukee Art Museum. A dramatic modern addition to the museum, called the Quadracci Pavilion, was completed in 2001.

Introduction

L ocated in the area of the United States known as the Midwest, Wisconsin has long been noted for its dairy farms and natural beauty. The slogan on the state's license plates, "America's Dairyland," displays Wisconsin's pride in its strong dairy industry. Manufacturing is also a significant part of Wisconsin's economy. The state is one of the nation's main producers of food products, machinery, and paper products.

During the last Ice Age, most of Wisconsin was covered by giant **glaciers**. As the glaciers moved across the land, they carved out one of the nation's most scenic states. Besides numerous lakes and rivers, Wisconsin features rolling hills, fertile valleys, and abundant forests.

The Bad River flows through a gorge in Copper Falls State Park in northern Wisconsin. The park was created in 1929.

Dairy farms are a common sight in Wisconsin, especially in the southern two-thirds of the state. Dairy makes up the largest segment of Wisconsin's agricultural industry.

Today, Wisconsin is still in many ways a rural state with a strong agricultural base. The larger cities, such as Milwaukee, Madison, Green Bay, and Racine, are urban places with strong roots in history. Many larger cities are concentrated in the southeastern part of the state. Dairy farming is concentrated in the southwest.

For much of its history, Wisconsin has been considered one of the nation's most **progressive** states. Many social, educational, and political **reforms** that spread throughout the United States began in Wisconsin. In about 1900, the Progressive movement began in the state, resulting in the passage of liberal legislation. The first successful worker's compensation law was passed in the state in 1911. A major figure in the Progressive movement was Robert M. La Follette Sr., who was born in Primrose. He served Wisconsin as a U.S. representative, U.S. senator, and governor.

Where Is Wisconsin?

Wisconsin is located in the north-central portion of the United States. Lake Superior borders it to the northwest for about 150 miles, and Lake Michigan borders it to the east for approximately 425 miles. The state is bordered by Illinois to the south, Michigan to the northeast, Iowa to the southwest, and Minnesota to the west. Bayfield **Peninsula** in northwest Wisconsin juts into Lake Superior, which is the largest freshwater lake in the world. Twenty-one islands in Lake Superior called the Apostle Islands make up a national lakeshore found off Bayfield Peninsula. The Door Peninsula, on the state's northeastern coast, extends into Lake Michigan.

Wisconsin's beautiful scenery and recreation areas attract millions of visitors each year. With more than 15,000 lakes and thousands of rivers, the state draws many people who enjoy fishing, boating, swimming, and other water sports. Skiing, tobogganing, and ice boating are popular winter pastimes in Wisconsin.

The Apostle Islands National Lakeshore is located on 21 islands in Lake Superior. Twelve miles of land on Wisconsin's northwest coast are also part of the national lakeshore.

General Mitchell International Airport in Milwaukee is the largest airport in Wisconsin. Ten airlines provide service to U.S. and other destinations. For those traveling by bus, there is also a Greyhound Terminal in Milwaukee, with buses going to many of the cities in the state. Other bus lines also serve the state. Train travelers can take several routes into the state. Highways out of Wisconsin connect to several large cities in the United States. The State Trunk Highway system includes approximately 11,800 miles of roadways and 4,900 bridges. This system makes up about 10 percent of all roads in the state, but it carries 60 percent of all traffic. The main highway, Interstate 94, connects Milwaukee with Chicago to the south. I-94 then runs diagonally across the state, connecting with the Twin Cities of Minnesota.

With its many rivers and lakes, Wisconsin is a popular place for those who enjoy fishing. Some 1.4 million people catch 88 million fish in the state each year.

Wisconsin is nicknamed the Badger State. Early miners in the state often dug homes or tunnels out of hillsides, like badgers.

The state was named for its main river, which was called "Ouisconsin" in early records. Some believe the name came from an American Indian word meaning either "grassy place" or "gathering of waters."

General Mitchell International Airport serves close to 10 million passengers every year.

The Door Peninsula, an 80-mile-long piece of land between Green Bay and Lake Michigan, is a popular vacation area.

Nearly 400 lake associations exist in Wisconsin. These are usually voluntary organizations that work to protect and improve the lake.

Mapping  Wisconsin

The 430-mile-long Wisconsin River is the longest river in the state. It begins at the Michigan border and flows south. When it meets the Baraboo mountain range, the river turns west and runs into the Mississippi River on the state's western border. Other rivers in the state include the Chippewa and St. Croix. Major lakes include Lake Winnebago, Petenwell Lake, and Lake Chippewa.

Sites and Symbols

STATE SEAL
Wisconsin

STATE FLAG
Wisconsin

STATE BIRD
Robin

STATE ANIMAL
Badger

STATE FLOWER
Wood violet

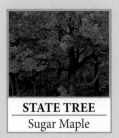

STATE TREE
Sugar Maple

Nickname The Badger State

Motto Forward

Song "On, Wisconsin!" by William T. Purdy, J. S. Hubbard, and Charles D. Rosa.

Entered the Union May 29, 1848, as the 30th state

Capital Madison

Population (2010 Census) 5,686,986 Ranked 20th state

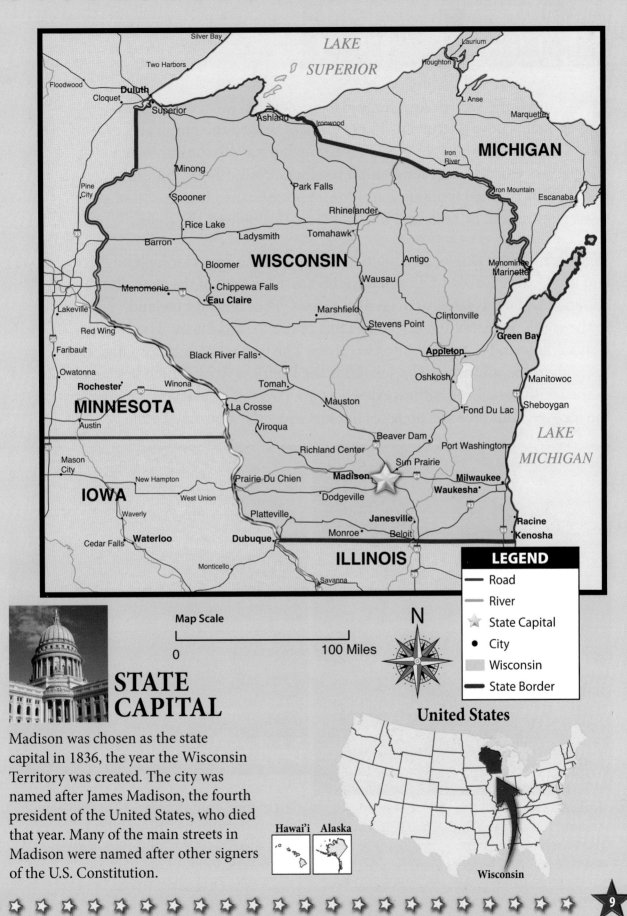

LAKE SUPERIOR

MICHIGAN

WISCONSIN

MINNESOTA

IOWA

ILLINOIS

LAKE MICHIGAN

Silver Bay · Two Harbors · Floodwood · Duluth · Cloquet · Superior · Ashland · Ironwood · Laurium · Houghton · L'Anse · Marquette · Iron River · Iron Mountain · Escanaba · Pine City · Minong · Spooner · Park Falls · Rhinelander · Antigo · Menominee · Marinette · Rice Lake · Ladysmith · Tomahawk · Wausau · Barron · Bloomer · Chippewa Falls · Menomonie · Eau Claire · Marshfield · Clintonville · Lakeville · Red Wing · Faribault · Stevens Point · Green Bay · Owatonna · Winona · Black River Falls · Appleton · Rochester · Tomah · Oshkosh · Manitowoc · Mauston · Fond Du Lac · Sheboygan · Austin · La Crosse · Viroqua · Mason City · Richland Center · Beaver Dam · Port Washington · New Hampton · Prairie Du Chien · Sun Prairie · Madison · Milwaukee · Waverly · West Union · Dodgeville · Waukesha · Waterloo · Cedar Falls · Platteville · Janesville · Racine · Dubuque · Monroe · Beloit · Kenosha · Monticello · Savanna

LEGEND

— Road
— River
⭐ State Capital
• City
Wisconsin
— State Border

Map Scale
0   100 Miles

N

United States

Hawai'i   Alaska

Wisconsin

STATE CAPITAL

Madison was chosen as the state capital in 1836, the year the Wisconsin Territory was created. The city was named after James Madison, the fourth president of the United States, who died that year. Many of the main streets in Madison were named after other signers of the U.S. Constitution.

9

The Land

During the last Ice Age, huge glaciers covered most of the land that is now Wisconsin. These glaciers shaped the physical features of much of the Midwest, including Wisconsin. When the glaciers receded, they left behind boulders, cone-shaped mounds, piles of debris called moraines, and round ponds called kettles. All of these features can be seen in different places throughout the state.

Wisconsin is made up of two main land regions, the Superior Upland and the Central Lowland. Located in the northern part of the state, the Superior Upland is largely covered by forests. The Central Lowland, in the south, is part of the Interior Plains of the United States. The Central Lowland is divided into two areas. The first is the Eastern Lake Section, in the southeast. The second is the Driftless Area, which lies in the southwest. The Driftless Area was not covered by glaciers during the Ice Age. This area has no lakes but has wide, flat-bottomed valleys.

WISCONSIN DELLS

The Wisconsin Dells has cliffs that were created 15,000 years ago. A glacier turned the Wisconsin River into a new channel that cut through the center of a sandstone plain.

DEVIL'S LAKE STATE PARK

This state park, in southern Wisconsin, is part of the Central Lowland. The 360-acre lake was created by a glacier thousands of years ago. This is the most popular state park in Wisconsin.

APOSTLE ISLANDS

Located in Lake Superior, the Apostle Islands have numerous beaches, sea caves, and interesting cliff formations.

SUPERIOR UPLAND

The Superior Upland covers the northern third of the state. Forests make up much of the region, as well as hundreds of lakes and a low plain interspersed with hills.

Timms Hill is the state's highest point, with an elevation of 1,951 feet. It is located in the north-central part of the state. The lowest point, at 579 feet above sea level, is along the Lake Michigan shoreline.

The Superior Upland is part of the Canadian Shield, a huge mass of ancient rock that also covers about half of Canada.

Lake Winnebago, the largest lake in the state, has an area of 137,708 acres.

The coastal landscape of northern Wisconsin near Lake Michigan includes the Niagara **Escarpment**, which is a limestone cliff along the east side of Green Bay.

An estimated 1 million people each year visit Peninsula State Park, which has eight miles of shoreline on the Door Peninsula.

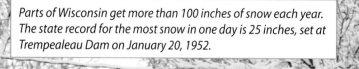

Parts of Wisconsin get more than 100 inches of snow each year. The state record for the most snow in one day is 25 inches, set at Trempealeau Dam on January 20, 1952.

Climate

Wisconsin winters are long and cold, and the summers are short and hot. In northern Wisconsin, temperatures may be lower than –40° Fahrenheit in the winter and higher than 90° F during the summer. The highest temperature ever recorded in Wisconsin was 114° F at the Wisconsin Dells on July 13, 1936. The lowest temperature was –55° F at Couderay on February 4, 1996.

The western and northern uplands get the most rain in the state, while Lake Michigan's shoreline receives the least precipitation. Rainfall is usually heaviest during the spring and summer, and thunderstorms are common during these seasons. Wisconsin has an average of 21 tornadoes each year.

Average Annual Precipitation Across Wisconsin

The average annual precipitation varies for different cities across Wisconsin. Why might Monroe get more rainfall than Green Bay?

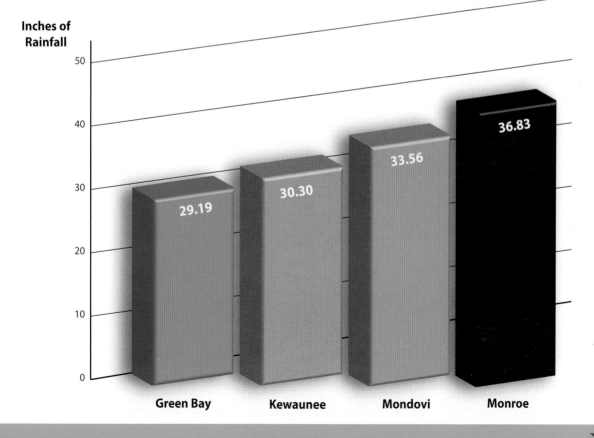

Natural Resources

Water and soil are Wisconsin's most valuable natural resources. Combined with a long growing season, these resources are key to the success of the dairy and other agricultural industries. The soil in Wisconsin is especially fertile in the southern part of the state. Meanwhile, the state's numerous rivers and lakes contain many fish for the commercial fishing industry. Commercial fishing has steadily increased in recent years thanks in part to fish restocking programs.

Wood from Wisconsin's trees is used to make many products, including paper and furniture. There are more than 65,000 workers in the state's forest products industry.

The fishing industry in Wisconsin arose years ago thanks to the rich supply of fish in Lake Michigan, Lake Superior, Green Bay, and many inland rivers. The state's ports today support both commercial and recreational fishing operations.

The lumber industry was very important to Wisconsin's economy beginning in the late 1800s. Millions of trees were cut down, however, and little was done at the time to replant them. As a result, many of the forests in Wisconsin suffered from **deforestation**. Trees are still important to the state. The northern section of the state is the most heavily forested, and millions of feet of lumber are produced each year from the state's hardwoods and softwoods. Wisconsin's forests are also important for tourism and recreation.

Wisconsin is rich in nonfuel minerals, such as lime, sand, gravel, and crushed stone. The state also has deposits of metallic minerals such as copper and zinc. However, these have not been extensively mined because of concerns about possible damage to the environment.

I DIDN'T KNOW THAT!

There are about 16 million acres of forests in Wisconsin. Almost 60 percent of this land is privately owned.

The number of fish in Lake Michigan decreased after the **sea lamprey** came to the Great Lakes in the 1800s. A restoration program has helped renew many fish **species**, including lake trout.

Crushed stone, sand, and gravel make up about three-fourths of the value of all minerals in Wisconsin.

A wide variety of wood products come from the state's forests. Much of the wood is used to make paper.

An estimated 2,500 to 3,000 nonmetallic mine sites are found in Wisconsin.

Wisconsin has a state soil, Antigo silt loam. It was named after the city of Antigo.

The most deadly forest fire in U.S. history took place in northeastern Wisconsin on October 8, 1871. The entire town of Peshtigo burned down, and fire damage extended over a large portion of six counties.

Plants

Wisconsin was once almost entirely covered by forests, but settlers eventually cleared most of the forestland for lumber and agriculture. Through natural regrowth and reforestation, however, much of the state is now forested again. Hardwood trees, including maple, birch, oak, aspen, and elm, are most common. **Conifers** such as hemlock, balsam fir, and black spruce are also plentiful. Raspberry, chokecherry, blueberry, and beaked hazelnut shrubs grow in the state. In the prairie regions, various types of grasses thrive.

Many flowers bloom throughout Wisconsin. The state boasts more than 40 different kinds of orchids. Other flowers in the state include the wild rose and the pitcher plant. Some of Wisconsin's flowers are rare. The dwarf lake iris, which grows near the Lake Michigan shoreline, is **threatened** in Wisconsin.

SUGAR MAPLE TREE

The state tree of Wisconsin, the sugar maple, is known for its brilliant fall colors. The tree may live as long as 400 years.

WOOD VIOLET

The wood violet, which is Wisconsin's state flower, is commonly found in wet woods and meadows as well as along roadsides. It blooms from March to June.

PRAIRIE CONEFLOWER

This common wildflower blooms from June to September. It can grow as tall as 5 feet. American Indians used the flowers to make a yellow-orange dye.

TRILLIUM

The state wildflower, the trillium, blooms early in the spring on the woodland floor. It is easy to identify by its three white petals, which have pointed tips.

Blueberries grown in Wisconsin are ready to be picked in July.

Many types of mushrooms grow wild in Wisconsin. Morels, a popular type of mushroom, are found in orchards and at the bases of trees in other areas.

Yarrow is a **perennial** herb that is native to the state. The plant, which grows to about 3 feet tall, has small, brown seeds that may be difficult to see.

Seven plant species are considered threatened in Wisconsin. They include the prairie bush clover, pitcher's thistle, and eastern prairie fringed orchid.

Animals

White-tailed deer, chipmunks, beavers, raccoons, and cottontail rabbits are found throughout the state. The northern part of the state has coyotes, wolves, and porcupines. Black bears live in the forests, and minks, river otters, and muskrats can be found in wetland areas. Bald eagles and elk live in some parts of Wisconsin. The state's freshwater streams are home to various trout species, sturgeon, bass, northern pike, and muskellunge, or muskie. Wisconsin is also home to hundreds of types of birds, including blackbirds, finches, hawks, eagles, and owls.

A number of animal species are either threatened or **endangered** in Wisconsin. Among Wisconsin's endangered animals are the piping plover and gray wolf. A number of insect species are also endangered, including the Karner blue butterfly.

HONEYBEE

The honeybee is the state insect. When honeybees fly from flower to flower looking for nectar, pollen sticks to them. The pollen then rubs off, fertilizing flowers.

CHIPMUNK

Chipmunks are small mammals, about the size of an orange. They carry food in their large cheek pouches.

ROBIN

The robin is the state bird of Wisconsin. It is known for its red breast, and its appearance is thought to be a sign of spring.

BLACK BEAR

The black bear is one of Wisconsin's largest native mammals. Adult males can weigh 350 pounds. They can run at speeds faster than 30 miles per hour.

I DIDN'T KNOW THAT!

The white-tailed deer is the state wildlife animal. Explorers in the 1600s reported seeing deer throughout the region that is now Wisconsin, especially in the south.

In 1985, the American water spaniel was adopted as Wisconsin's state dog. This type of dog is very friendly and has a keen sense of smell.

The state fish is the muskellunge. It is a large fish that can weigh almost 70 pounds.

A number of types of fish have been introduced into Lake Michigan, including coho and chinook salmon.

Lake Winnebago has one of the world's largest self-sustaining populations of lake sturgeon.

The dairy cow is Wisconsin's official state domesticated animal. There are more than 1.2 million cows in the state.

Tourism

Tourists come to Wisconsin to enjoy the impressive scenery and recreational areas. Wisconsin has 13 state forests where visitors can camp, picnic, and participate in water sports. The two national forests in the state, Chequamegon National Forest and Nicolet National Forest, are ideal for hiking, camping, and fishing. The Wisconsin Dells area is one of the largest tourist attractions in the Midwest.

Taliesin, the estate of well-known architect Frank Lloyd Wright, who was born in Wisconsin, is another popular tourist attraction. It is located near Spring Green. There are many fascinating museums in Wisconsin. Little Norway is an outdoor museum set up like a small Norwegian village. The National Railroad Museum in Green Bay is full of information on the history of railroads. The Wisconsin Maritime Museum, in Manitowoc, has a restored World War II submarine, a recreated 19th-century ship-building town, and a gallery of model ships.

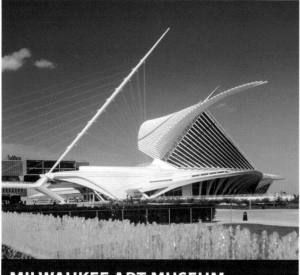

MILWAUKEE ART MUSEUM

The Milwaukee Art Museum has 20,000 works of art. Among the famous artists in the museum's collection are Georgia O'Keeffe, Winslow Homer, Edgar Degas, and Pablo Picasso.

THE DOOR PENINSULA

The Door Peninsula, which extends into Lake Michigan, is a popular vacation spot. It is lined with lighthouses, most built during the 1800s. It has also 300 miles of shoreline, many beaches, and orchards.

NICOLET NATIONAL FOREST

This national forest covers more than 660,000 acres in northeast Wisconsin. Visitors can hike, bike, camp, boat, and fish in the forest, which was established in 1933.

WISCONSIN DELLS

Visitors to the Wisconsin Dells, one of the state's most popular attractions, can enjoy scenic views of cliffs and sandstone formations. The area is also known for its many water parks.

I DIDN'T KNOW THAT!

The Circus World Museum in Baraboo has a huge collection of circus items, including more than 200 original wagons and other vehicles, circus posters, and equipment once owned by circus performers.

The nation's largest water park, Noah's Ark, is in the Wisconsin Dells. It has 49 water rides and two giant wave pools.

Many boat tours provide tourists with an interesting view of the Wisconsin Dells.

Tourists spend more than $12 billion in Wisconsin each year. The tourist industry provides nearly 300,000 full-time jobs to Wisconsinites.

The Harley-Davidson Museum in Milwaukee has exhibits tracing the history of the motorcycle company, which was founded in 1903.

Industry

The dairy industry continues to play a significant role in Wisconsin's economy, and the state is a leading producer of natural cheese, butter, and milk. In recent decades, however, manufacturing has become a major source of income in the state. Of particular importance is the manufacture of machinery, especially items used in agriculture, construction, and mining. Other products manufactured in Wisconsin are engines and turbines, electrical equipment, medical equipment, and household appliances.

Industries in Wisconsin
Value of Goods and Services in Millions of Dollars

Government makes up a significant portion of Wisconsin's economy. What types of jobs are included in government? What do government workers do for the state and its people?

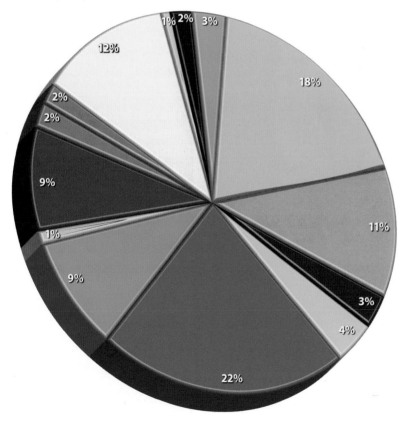

LEGEND

Agriculture, Forestry, and Fishing	$3,941
* Mining	$454
Utilities	$4,531
Construction	$8,202
Manufacturing	$42,259
Wholesale and Retail Trade	$27,373
Transportation	$7,023
Media and Entertainment	$9,218
Finance, Insurance, and Real Estate	$51,975
Professional and Technical Services	$21,217
Education	$2,306
Health Care	$22,082
Hotels and Restaurants	$5,539
Other Services	$5,898
Government	$27,493
TOTAL	**$239,061**

*Less than 1%. Percentages may not add to 100 because of rounding.

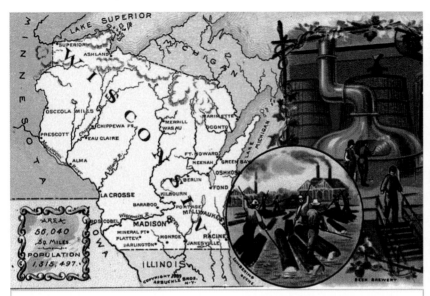

Trading cards from the late 1800s highlighted major industries in Wisconsin, such as lumber and beer manufacturing.

Wisconsin's forest products industries employ more than 65,000 people. These industries account for 14.4 percent of all of the state's manufacturing jobs. Wisconsin is a major producer of paper and paper products in the United States. In fact, the state makes more paper than any other state in the nation. Paper mills are found around Milwaukee and in the Lake Winnebago region. The state's lumber industry is also strong.

In the early 1900s, Wisconsin was the leading lumber state in the country.

Colby and brick cheese were first made in Wisconsin.

The first ice cream sundae is believed to have been made in Two Rivers in 1881. The first malted milk was sold to the public in the 1880s in Racine.

The state's first cheese factory opened in Ladoga in 1864.

The first hydroelectric power plant in the United States began operation on the Fox River at Appleton in 1882.

Wisconsin has been the leading paper-making state for more than 50 years. The forest industry also manufactures pulp, wooden furniture, plywood, and other wooden products.

Goods and Services

Wisconsin has approximately 13,000 dairy farms. More than 1.2 million cows produce an average of 20,070 pounds of milk each per year. Wisconsin cheese-makers use some 90 percent of this milk to produce cheese at 138 plants. The state also produces most of the condensed milk and canned evaporated milk in the nation. Other food products made in Wisconsin include canned fruits and vegetables. Wisconsin's farmers grow kidney beans, potatoes, and soybeans in large quantities. They sell chickens, hogs, and eggs. The state is a leading producer of corn and hay, which are chiefly used as feed for livestock. Wisconsin has been called the beer capital of the nation because it has a long history of brewing beer. The Miller Brewing Company was started in Milwaukee in 1858. Now part of MillerCoors, it has brewing facilities in Milwaukee and Chippewa Falls.

Wisconsin's dairy industry produces 26 billion pounds of milk and 2.6 billion pounds of cheese each year.

Cranberries are Wisconsin's leading fruit crop in terms of both value and acreage. The state grows 60 percent of the nation's cranberries.

The fur industry, which played a large role in the history of Wisconsin, is still present in the state. Fur farms have replaced most of the trapping of fur-bearing animals. The fishing industry is small but significant in Wisconsin.

Many major companies have their headquarters in Wisconsin. The Kohler Company, which manufactures plumbing equipment and fixtures, is based in the city of Kohler. The department store chain Kohl's is based in Menomonee Falls, and the Lands' End clothing company is located in Dodgeville. S.C. Johnson & Son, which makes household cleaning supplies, is another well-known Wisconsin company.

American Indians

The first people to live in the land that became Wisconsin were prehistoric American Indians. They are believed to have arrived more than 11,000 years ago. These early peoples were **nomadic**, and they hunted reindeer and other large animals. They also gathered plants. Later peoples who lived in the area included a group that scientists now call the Mound Builders. They built large mounds of earth that are believed to have been used for ceremonies and burials. Some of the mounds have been found to contain items such as pottery and shells.

In the 1600s, when explorers of European heritage came to the area, the Winnebago Indians lived in wigwams. These shelters were built with wooden frames that had animal skins stretched over them.

When the first European explorers arrived in the area in the 1600s, they found a number of groups in the region. Among them were the Menominee, the Kickapoo, the Miami, the Ojibwe, who were also called the Chippewa, and the Winnebago, who were also called the Ho-chunk. In the early 1800s, other Indian groups entered Wisconsin, including the Oneida and the Stockbridge. As the years went on, Indian groups fought among themselves over control of the fur trade with the Europeans. Later, they also fought with the U.S. government and settlers from the eastern United States over control of the land.

A statue of Chief Oshkosh of the Menominee Indians stands in the city of Oshkosh. He helped his people negotiate treaties with the U.S. government in the 1800s.

I DIDN'T KNOW THAT!

Remains of some of the mounds made by the Mound Builders can still be found at many locations in Wisconsin. A number of the mounds are in the shape of animals, such as panthers, birds, and turtles.

In 1994, the Winnebago adopted Ho-chunk as their official name.

There are a number of Indian **reservations** in Wisconsin today. The tribes who live on them include the Menominee, the Ojibwe, the Potawatomi, the Stockbridge, the Munsee, and the Oneida.

Traditional and contemporary Indian culture is celebrated at Wisconsin's Indian Summer Festival and Winter Pow Wow, both held in Milwaukee.

Father Jacques Marquette and Louis Joliet traveled by canoe into Green Bay in 1673. From there, they continued down the Wisconsin River for seven days until they reached the Mississippi.

Explorers and Missionaries

Jean Nicolet, a French explorer, may have been the first European to visit the land that is now Wisconsin. He arrived in the northeast in 1634 while searching for a route across North America to China. The French fur trader Médard Chouart, sieur des Groseilliers, and his brother-in-law, Pierre Esprit Radisson, later explored the area around Lake Superior in 1658. Missionaries also came to the area to teach Christianity to the Indians. Father René Ménard is believed to have been the first missionary in Wisconsin. He arrived in the area in 1660 but disappeared the following year. The first permanent mission in Wisconsin was founded by Father Claude Allouez in 1665 near De Pere.

Two French explorers, Father Jacques Marquette and Louis Joliet, crossed Wisconsin in 1673. In the following years, there was an active fur trade between Europeans and Indians. From 1754 to 1763, Great Britain and France, with their Indian allies, engaged in the French and Indian War for control of eastern North America. In 1763, France was forced to give Britain almost all of its territory east of the Mississippi River, including Wisconsin. In 1783, after the American Revolution, Britain surrendered the land to the United States. After the War of 1812, people from the eastern United States began to settle in Wisconsin in greater numbers.

Timeline of Settlement

Early Exploration

1634 French explorer Jean Nicolet is the first European known to visit the area, arriving near Green Bay.

1658 French fur traders Pierre Esprit Radisson and Médard Chouart, sieur des Groseilliers, explore the area around Lake Superior.

1660 Father René Ménard arrives in the region.

1665 Father Claude Allouez establishes a mission near De Pere.

1673 Jacques Marquette and Louis Joliet cross Wisconsin by canoe.

Conflicts

1754 The French and Indian War begins between France and Great Britain.

1763 The British win the French and Indian War. They gain control of the region that includes Wisconsin.

1783 As a result of the American Revolution, the new United States officially gains what is now Wisconsin from Great Britain.

1795 French Canadian fur traders establish a post near the Menominee River that eventually becomes Milwaukee.

Territory and Statehood

1800 Wisconsin becomes part of the Indiana Territory.

1814 Following the War of 1812, the U.S. government begins to establish forts in the area.

1829–1833 The United States signs a series of treaties with Indian groups in the Wisconsin area.

1832 The Black Hawk War ends Indian resistance to white settlement.

1836 The Wisconsin Territory is formed.

1836 Madison is chosen as the territorial capital.

1848 Wisconsin becomes a state.

Early Settlers

I n the 1820s, many settlers from nearby territories and states flocked to Wisconsin because of the lead deposits found in the southwestern area. The discovery sparked a "lead rush" and later attracted miners from such distant regions as Cornwall, England. At first, the miners lived in crude shelters, such as dug-out holes.

Map of Settlements and Resources in Early Wisconsin

5 *Fountain City, originally called Holmes' Landing, is founded by Thomas Holmes in 1839. Rich agricultural land draws immigrants from such places as Germany, Switzerland, and Norway.*

1 *Jean Nicolet establishes a fur trading post at Green Bay in 1634. Fur trader Charles de Langlade, later called the "Father of Wisconsin," becomes one of the first permanent settlers of European descent there in 1765.*

6 *Fur traders come to the area that develops into Oshkosh in the early 1800s, but the city eventually grows as a result of the lumber industry in the region. It is incorporated as a city in 1853.*

2 *French Canadian fur traders establish a trading post near the Menominee River in 1795. Three separate towns develop in the area. They officially unite in 1846 as the city of Milwaukee.*

3 *In 1832, settlers from New York State arrive near where the Root River empties into Lake Michigan. The settlement officially becomes Racine in 1841. The town is an important site on the Underground Railroad, as residents help slaves from the South escape to freedom in Canada.*

4 *Politician James Doty purchases 1,000 acres of swamp and forestland in 1836, intending to build a city on the site. It becomes Madison, which is chosen as the capital of the Wisconsin Territory.*

Scale

0   100 Miles

N

LEGEND	
🏠 Settlement	🪶 Farming
— River	▢ Wisconsin
🦫 Fur	▬ State Border
🪵 Wood	

Soon, settlements were established as land was cleared and houses and roads were built. The increasing number of settlers led to conflicts with the Indians living there. Between 1829 and 1833, the U.S. government signed a series of treaties with the Indian groups that helped open the land for settlers. Indian resistance to settlers ended with the Black Hawk War of 1832. Black Hawk, an Indian chief, was attempting to lead his people to Illinois. They fled to Wisconsin when U.S. troops came after them, and they were finally defeated at the Battle of Bad Axe on the banks of the Mississippi.

After this, more new settlers came to Wisconsin, mostly from eastern states, especially New York. They settled along the shores of Lake Michigan and became farmers or traders. In 1836, the Wisconsin Territory was formed. It included Wisconsin, Iowa, Minnesota, and parts of North and South Dakota. In 1838, the territory was made smaller when the land west of the Mississippi River became the Iowa Territory. More people came to Wisconsin during this period, including many from Europe. Large numbers of people from Germany, Scotland, Ireland, Wales, Switzerland, and Norway settled in the area.

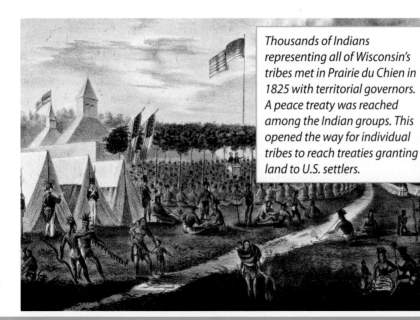

Thousands of Indians representing all of Wisconsin's tribes met in Prairie du Chien in 1825 with territorial governors. A peace treaty was reached among the Indian groups. This opened the way for individual tribes to reach treaties granting land to U.S. settlers.

I DIDN'T KNOW THAT!

The first capital of the Wisconsin Territory was the small settlement of Belmont in the southwest. The legislature moved to Burlington, now in Iowa, before establishing its permanent residence in Madison.

In the 1830s, people in Wisconsin began asking that railroad lines be built in the region. Soon, a number of railroads were chartered and many towns got new rail lines.

Between 1840 and 1850, Wisconsin's population increased from approximately 31,000 to 305,000. By 1900, the state was home to more than 2 million people.

Located near Belmont, First Capitol State Park was dedicated in 1924. The historic site features restored buildings that housed the original territory's government.

Iron mining began in Wisconsin in 1849. It was discontinued about 1965 because of competition from other states.

Notable People

Many notable Wisconsinites contributed to the development of their state and country. Major political leaders, activists, artists, architects, and scientists have called Wisconsin home.

**JOHN MUIR
(1838–1914)**

John Muir was born in Scotland. He and his family moved to a farm in Marquette County in 1849, when he was 11 years old. He enjoyed the wilderness and explored the area. After attending the University of Wisconsin, he traveled across the United States, settling in Yosemite Valley, California. Muir became a **conservationist**, concerned about protecting the environment. In 1890, he worked to have Congress create Yosemite National Park and Sequoia National Park. He also persuaded President Theodore Roosevelt to set aside land for national parks and forest preserves. In 1892, Muir founded the Sierra Club, which still works today to protect the environment.

**ROBERT M. LA FOLLETTE SR.
(1855–1925)**

Robert M. La Follette Sr. was born in Primrose. He became a lawyer, as did his wife, Belle Case, who was the first woman to receive a law degree from the University of Wisconsin. La Follette served as a U.S. representative from Wisconsin from 1885 to 1891. He was also the state's governor from 1901 to 1906, and a U.S. senator from 1906 until his death. In 1924, he unsuccessfully ran for president as the candidate of the Progressive Party. Throughout his career, he backed such ideas as making business and politics more honest, protecting state forests, and paying government workers based on merit and not their social standing.

FRANK LLOYD WRIGHT
(1867–1959)

Frank Lloyd Wright was born in Richland County. He became an influential architect and the leader of the Prairie School of architecture. He designed buildings that reflected the flat land of the Midwestern prairies. His buildings mixed modern styles with nature and light. Taliesin, a house he built for himself near Spring Green, is one of his best-known designs.

GOLDA MEIR
(1898–1978)

Golda Meir was born in Ukraine. Her family moved to Milwaukee in 1906. She became a teacher there, got married, and then moved with her husband to Palestine in the Middle East. She worked for the founding of Israel, a Jewish nation. After it was created, she served in the Israeli parliament, then became the country's prime minister from 1969 to 1973.

WILLIAM H. REHNQUIST
(1924–2005)

William H. Rehnquist was born in Milwaukee. He served in World War II, then became a lawyer. In January 1972, he became a justice on the U.S. Supreme Court. In 1986, when the chief justice retired, Rehnquist replaced him. Known as a conservative, he served as chief justice until his death.

Georgia O'Keeffe (1887–1986) was born in Sun Prairie. She became a famous painter, especially known for her paintings of large flowers and the Southwestern desert.

John Bardeen (1908–1991) was born in Madison. He is the only person who has won the Nobel Prize in Physics twice, in 1956 for inventing the **transistor** and in 1972 for a theory of **superconductivity**.

Population

Wisconsin had a population of almost 5.7 million people in the 2010 Census. Between 2000 and 2010, the state's population increased by 6 percent. Approximately two-thirds of Wisconsinites live in urban areas. Milwaukee is the largest city in the state, with almost 600,000 people. However, the population of Milwaukee decreased in the late 20th and early 21st century as people moved to nearby suburban areas. Besides Milwaukee, Wisconsin has two other cities with populations of more than 100,000. Madison has 233,000 people, and Green Bay has 104,000. The next largest cities are Kenosha and Racine.

Wisconsin Population 1950–2010

The population of Wisconsin grew by about 1 million people between 1950 and 1970. That was a larger increase than in each of the next two 20-year periods. What factors may account for the different rates of population growth?

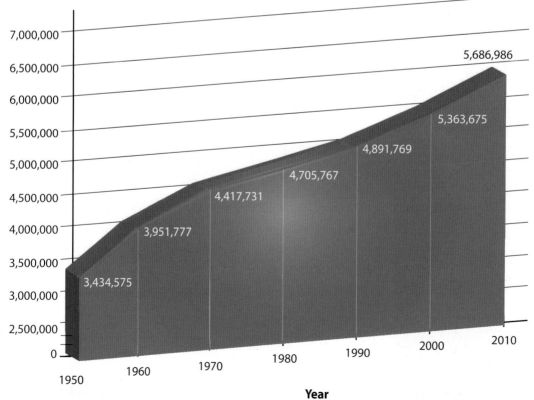

Number of People

3,434,575
3,951,777
4,417,731
4,705,767
4,891,769
5,363,675
5,686,986

Year

About 23 percent of Wisconsin's population is under 18 years of age. More than 13 percent is 65 years old or older. Both of these figures are close to the national averages. About nine out of 10 Wisconsites are of European heritage, and 6.2 percent of the population is African American. Hispanic Americans make up more than 5 percent of the population.

The University of Wisconsin System has 13 four-year universities and 13 two-year colleges. It is one of the largest systems of public higher education in the United States, with almost 182,000 students. The main campus is located in Madison. Among the private schools of higher education in Wisconsin is Beloit College. Founded in 1846, it is the oldest continuously operated college in Wisconsin.

Capitol Square in downtown Madison is a popular spot for public gatherings. People there attend outdoor concerts, food festivals, art shows, and other events.

The largest American Indian groups in Wisconsin are the Ojibwe, the Oneida, and the Menominee.

Approximately 85 percent of Wisconsinites over the age of 25 have graduated from high school.

The first kindergarten in the United States was opened in 1856 in Watertown. The word *kindergarten* means "children's garden" in German.

The University of Wisconsin was the first in the nation to offer extension courses, which are classes for people who are not enrolled as regular students. The state also had the country's first vocational schools.

Wisconsin's state capitol building, where the state legislature meets, was built between 1906 and 1917. It cost $7.25 million to construct.

Politics and Government

Wisconsin's government, like the federal government of the United States, is divided into three branches. They are the executive, the legislative, and the judicial branches. The executive branch, led by the governor, is responsible for making sure state laws are carried out. Among the governor's many responsibilities is proposing the state budget. The governor and lieutenant governor, along with other public officials such as the secretary of state and attorney general, serve four-year terms. The legislative branch is divided into two parts. The Assembly has 99 members who are elected to two-year terms. The Senate has 33 members who are elected to four-year terms. Together, they form the State Legislature, which creates Wisconsin's laws. The judicial branch interprets laws and governs the court system. Seven judges rule on cases in the state's Supreme Court, which is the highest court in the state. These judges are elected to 10-year terms. There are also lower-level courts in Wisconsin.

The state is known for two political movements that began in the early 20th century. At the time, rich and powerful people controlled the timber and railway industries in the state, and many people felt that reforms were needed. This led to the Progressive movement and the Wisconsin Idea. The Wisconsin Idea was an effort to bring together all of the state's resources, including those of education and government, to solve social, economic, and political problems in the state. Leaders hoped that experts would study problems and figure out the best way to deal with them.

I DIDN'T KNOW THAT!

Wisconsin's state song is called "On, Wisconsin!"

Here are the words to the song:

On, Wisconsin! On, Wisconsin!
Grand old badger state!
We, thy loyal sons and
* daughters,*
Hail thee, good and great.
On, Wisconsin! On, Wisconsin!
Champion of the right,
"Forward," our motto
God will give thee might!

The dome of the state capitol building reaches a height of 265 feet. It is the only granite dome in the United States.

Cultural Groups

Most of the people from other countries who settled in Wisconsin came from Europe, especially Germany. People came from Poland, Scandinavia, and England as well. Within the United States, many newcomers moved to Wisconsin from New York, New England, and the South. Early settlers created their own communities, and their descendants have continued to practice many of their traditions. Some ethnic groups in Wisconsin hold annual festivals to celebrate their culture. Each year in Stoughton, people of Norwegian descent hold the Syttende Mai festival, which can be translated as "17th of May." People dress in traditional Norwegian costumes, watch and participate in folk dancing, and enjoy Norwegian food and music. There is also a contest for children, who compete to draw the ugliest troll.

Many of the people who settled on Washington Island, located northeast of the tip of the Door Peninsula, were Norwegian immigrants. They built a wooden church there modeled after the type found in Norway.

Powwows and other gatherings are held by different Indian groups throughout Wisconsin. Milwaukee has held its Indian Summer Festival every year since 1987.

At Milwaukee's Polish Fest, a piano contest is held for young people, who must play the works of Polish composer Frédéric Chopin.

The polka, a Central European dance, is the state dance of Wisconsin.

Stoughton has celebrated Syttende Mai since 1868, which was a peak period of Norwegian immigration to Wisconsin.

Pierogi are a popular Polish food. They are dumplings containing fillings such as potatoes, cabbage, or cheese.

Thousands of people from across the world, including Germany, flock to German Fest in Milwaukee each July.

In New Glarus, people of Swiss background hold the annual Wilhelm Tell Festival. German Fest, held annually in Milwaukee, is a celebration of German culture that lasts for several days. German musicians and dancers perform, and people sample traditional German food such as schnitzel and strudel. Milwaukee also hosts Polish Fest, a celebration held for three days each June. There are Polish storytellers, crafts, dance contests, food, and history exhibits.

Milwaukee has celebrated the Holiday Folk Fair International since 1943. The fair, which is one of the largest multicultural celebrations in the United States, promotes racial, ethnic, and cultural understanding. It also highlights the contributions that people of various ethnic backgrounds have made to Wisconsin.

Arts and Entertainment

Wisconsin is home to many arts groups. Milwaukee, for example, has a symphony orchestra, a ballet company, and the Florentine Opera Company. The Milwaukee Art Museum features an excellent collection of European and American art. A number of notable writers are from Wisconsin. The novelist and playwright Thornton Wilder was born in Madison in 1897. He won Pulitzer Prizes for his novel *The Bridge of San Luis Rey* and for his plays *Our Town* and *The Skin of Our Teeth*. Children's author Laura Ingalls Wilder was born in Pepin in 1867. Her family's home there became the setting for her first book, *Little House in the Big Woods*. More recently, Kevin Henkes was born in Racine in 1960 and lives in Madison. His popular children's books include *Lilly's Purple Plastic Purse, Chester's Way*, and *Julius, the Baby of the World*.

Musician and singer Steve Miller was born in Milwaukee and attended the University of Wisconsin. In 1967, he formed the Steve Miller Band, which is still touring today.

Wisconsin has many fine **bluegrass** musicians. The Southern Wisconsin Bluegrass Music Association, established in 1983, sponsors bluegrass concerts in Wisconsin and other parts of the Midwest. Les Paul, an influential jazz and country guitarist, was born in Waukesha in 1915. He helped to develop the solid-body electric guitar and different recording techniques. Big-band leader Woody Herman was born in Milwaukee in 1913. Current actors from Wisconsin include Heather Graham, Mark Ruffalo, Tyne Daly, and Tony Shaloub.

The circus business in Wisconsin began in the 1800s. In 1847, Edmund and Jeremiah Mabie moved the winter location of their U.S. Olympic Circus to Delavan. Many other circuses began spending their winters in the state. The Ringling Brothers Circus was founded in Baraboo in 1884. In 1907, the Ringlings bought another major circus, the Barnum & Bailey Circus. The two circuses were combined in 1919. The Ringling Bros. and Barnum & Bailey Circus still tours the globe, billing itself as the "Greatest Show on Earth."

Actress Heather Graham was born in Milwaukee. She has appeared in more than 50 films, including Hope Springs *and* Anger Management.

Sports

Wisconsin's sports fans have plenty of action to enjoy. The state has three professional sports teams. The Milwaukee Brewers are the state's Major League Baseball team. They began as a team in Seattle, Washington, in 1969, then moved to Milwaukee in 1970. The Milwaukee Bucks have been playing in the National Basketball Association since 1968. The Bucks won the league championship in their third season, with basketball legends Oscar Robertson and Kareem Abdul-Jabbar playing for the team.

The Green Bay Packers are one of the oldest franchises in the National Football League, or NFL. Founded in 1919, the Packers are the only professional sports team in the nation that is publicly owned. The Packers have won 13 championships, more than any other team in the history of the NFL, including the 2011 Super Bowl. From 1959 to 1967, the Packers were coached by Vince Lombardi, who led the team to seven titles. Lombardi became legendary for his determination to win. The NFL's Super Bowl trophy is named after him.

First baseman Prince Fielder has played for the Milwaukee Brewers since 2005. He holds the team record for most home runs in a season, hitting 50 homers in 2007.

Lake Michigan and many inland lakes in Wisconsin are popular locations for water sports such as sailing, boating, waterskiing, and windsurfing. Boat races, called regattas, are held on Lake Winnebago each year. In the winter, snowmobiling, iceboating, sledding, downhill skiing, cross-country skiing, and ice skating are popular sports for Wisconsinites and tourists.

Quarterback Aaron Rodgers led the Green Bay Packers to victory in the Super Bowl in February 2011. The Packers beat the Pittsburgh Steelers by a score of 31-25.

I DIDN'T KNOW THAT!

The largest cross-country ski race in North America takes place in Wisconsin. The American Birkebeiner is held between Cable and Hayward.

The University of Wisconsin Badgers are one of the top-ranked college football teams in the nation.

Wisconsin native and speedskater Eric Heiden won five Olympic gold medals in 1980. After his competitive career ended, he went to medical school and became a doctor.

Fans of the Green Bay Packers are often referred to as "cheeseheads." Many wear hats shaped like wedges of cheese.

National Averages Comparison

T he United States is a federal republic, consisting of fifty states and the District of Columbia. Alaska and Hawai'i are the only non-contiguous, or non-touching, states in the nation. Today, the United States of America is the third-largest country in the world in population. The United States Census Bureau takes a census, or count of all the people, every ten years. It also regularly collects other kinds of data about the population and the economy. How does Wisconsin compare to the national average?

Comparison Chart

United States 2010 Census Data *	USA	Wisconsin
Admission to Union	NA	May 29, 1848
Land Area (in square miles)	3,537,438.44	54,310.10
Population Total	308,745,538	5,686,986
Population Density (people per square mile)	87.28	104.71
Population Percentage Change (April 1, 2000, to April 1, 2010)	9.7%	6.0%
White Persons (percent)	72.4%	86.2%
Black Persons (percent)	12.6%	6.3%
American Indian and Alaska Native Persons (percent)	0.9%	1.0%
Asian Persons (percent)	4.8%	2.3%
Native Hawaiian and Other Pacific Islander Persons (percent)	0.2%	—
Some Other Race (percent)	6.2%	2.4%
Persons Reporting Two or More Races (percent)	2.9%	1.8%
Persons of Hispanic or Latino Origin (percent)	16.3%	5.9%
Not of Hispanic or Latino Origin (percent)	83.7%	94.1%
Median Household Income	$52,029	$52,103
Percentage of People Age 25 or Over Who Have Graduated from High School	80.4%	85.1%

*All figures are based on the 2010 United States Census, with the exception of the last two items.

How to Improve My Community

Strong communities make strong states. Think about what features are important in your community. What do you value? Education? Health? Forests? Safety? Beautiful spaces? Government works to help citizens create ideal living conditions that are fair to all by providing services in communities. Consider what changes you could make in your community. How would they improve your state as a whole? Using this concept web as a guide, write a report that outlines the features you think are most important in your community and what improvements could be made. A strong state needs strong communities.

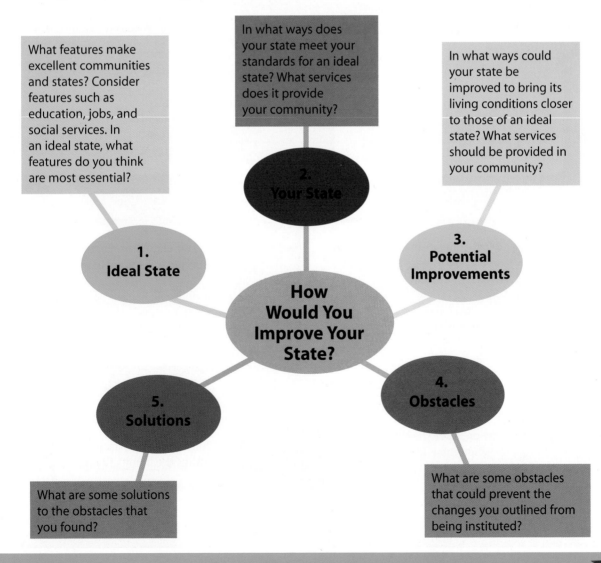

What features make excellent communities and states? Consider features such as education, jobs, and social services. In an ideal state, what features do you think are most essential?

In what ways does your state meet your standards for an ideal state? What services does it provide your community?

In what ways could your state be improved to bring its living conditions closer to those of an ideal state? What services should be provided in your community?

2. Your State

1. Ideal State

3. Potential Improvements

How Would You Improve Your State?

5. Solutions

4. Obstacles

What are some solutions to the obstacles that you found?

What are some obstacles that could prevent the changes you outlined from being instituted?

Exercise Your Mind!

Think about these questions and then use your research skills to find the answers and learn more fascinating facts about Wisconsin. A teacher, librarian, or parent may be able to help you locate the best sources to use in your research.

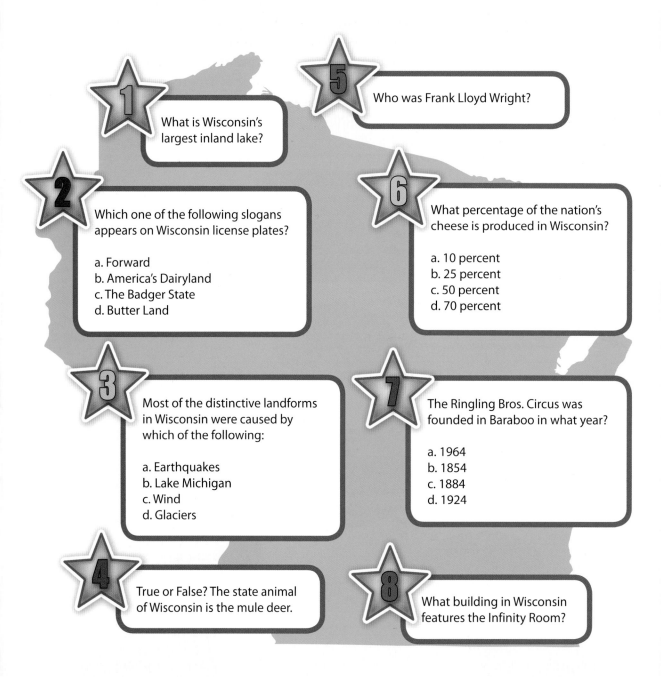

1 What is Wisconsin's largest inland lake?

2 Which one of the following slogans appears on Wisconsin license plates?

a. Forward
b. America's Dairyland
c. The Badger State
d. Butter Land

3 Most of the distinctive landforms in Wisconsin were caused by which of the following:

a. Earthquakes
b. Lake Michigan
c. Wind
d. Glaciers

4 True or False? The state animal of Wisconsin is the mule deer.

5 Who was Frank Lloyd Wright?

6 What percentage of the nation's cheese is produced in Wisconsin?

a. 10 percent
b. 25 percent
c. 50 percent
d. 70 percent

7 The Ringling Bros. Circus was founded in Baraboo in what year?

a. 1964
b. 1854
c. 1884
d. 1924

8 What building in Wisconsin features the Infinity Room?

Words to Know

bluegrass: a kind of country music

conifers: trees, such as evergreens and shrubs, that bear their seeds and pollen on separate, cone-shaped structures

conservationist: someone who tries to protect forests, wildlife, and other natural resources

deforestation: the cutting down and clearing away of trees

endangered: in danger of dying out

escarpment: a steep slope at the edge of a plateau

ginseng: a plant used for its medicinal properties

glaciers: large masses of slow-moving ice

nomadic: wandering from place to place with no permanent home

peninsula: a piece of land that is almost entirely surrounded by water

perennial: a plant with a life cycle of more than two years

progressive: striving toward better conditions in society and government

reforms: improvements made to correct something that is unsatisfactory

reservations: areas of land set aside by the government for American Indians

sea lamprey: an eel-like type of marine creature

species: a group of animals or plants that share the same characteristics and can mate

superconductivity: the property of some substances to transmit electricity, heat, or sound

threatened: at risk of becoming endangered

transistor: an electronic device that controls the flow of electric currents in such things as television sets and computers

Index

Log on to www.av2books.com

AV[2] by Weigl brings you media enhanced books that support active learning. Go to www.av2books.com, and enter the special code found on page 2 of this book. You will gain access to enriched and enhanced content that supplements and complements this book. Content includes video, audio, web links, quizzes, a slide show, and activities.

Audio
Listen to sections of the book read aloud.

Video
Watch informative video clips.

Embedded Weblinks
Gain additional information for research.

Try This!
Complete activities and hands-on experiments.

WHAT'S ONLINE?

Try This!	Embedded Weblinks	Video	EXTRA FEATURES
Test your knowledge of the state in a mapping activity.	Discover more attractions in Wisconsin.	Watch a video introduction to Wisconsin.	**Audio** Listen to sections of the book read aloud.
Find out more about precipitation in your city.	Learn more about the history of the state.	Watch a video about the features of the state.	
Plan what attractions you would like to visit in the state.	Learn the full lyrics of the state song.		**Key Words** Study vocabulary, and complete a matching word activity.
Learn more about the early natural resources of the state.			
Write a biography about a notable resident of Wisconsin.			**Slide Show** View images and captions, and prepare a presentation.
Complete an educational census activity.			**Quizzes** Test your knowledge.

AV[2] was built to bridge the gap between print and digital. We encourage you to tell us what you like and what you want to see in the future.
Sign up to be an AV[2] Ambassador at www.av2books.com/ambassador.